SNAKES

LIVING WILD

Published by Creative Education
P.O. Box 227, Mankato, Minnesota 56002
Creative Education is an imprint of The Creative Company
www.thecreativecompany.us

Design and production by Mary Herrmann
Art direction by Rita Marshall
Printed in the United States of America

Photographs by 123RF (Eric Chiang, Rusty Dodson, R L Hambley, Pavel Lebedinsky, Cosmin Manci, Enrique Ramos Lopez, Kristian Sekulic), Alamy (North Wind Picture Archives), Corbis (Brandon D. Cole, Michael & Patricia Fogden, Peter Ginter/Science Faction, Martin Harvey), Dreamstime (Andybutkaj, Bertrandb, Issalina, Mb-fotos, Pixart, Sharkegg), Getty Images (Tom Bean, DEA PICTURE LIBRARY, George Grall, Thad Samuels Abell Ii, Joel Sartore, Roy Toft), iStockphoto (John Bell, Karel Broz, Jake Holmes, Cindy Jen, Mark Kostich, David Parsons, Brad Phillips, Chanyut Sribua-rawd, Brenda A. Smith, Nico Smit, Jim Travis, Jeremy Wedel), Minden Pictures (Michael & Patricia Fogden, Pete Oxford), Jake Socha

Library of Congress Cataloging-in-Publication Data
Wimmer, Teresa, 1975–
Snakes / by Teresa Wimmer.
p. cm. — (Living wild)
Includes bibliographical references and index.
ISBN 978-1-58341-743-0
1. Snakes—Juvenile literature. I. Title. II. Series.

QL666.O6W466 2009
597.96—dc22   2008009506

First Edition
9 8 7 6 5 4 3 2 1

CREATIVE EDUCATION

SNAKES

Teresa Wimmer

On a warm morning in late spring, a prairie rattlesnake slithers out of its den. It has been inside

a dark crevice for six months, and the sudden, bright sunlight stings its sensitive eyes.

On a warm morning in late spring, a prairie rattlesnake slithers out of its den. It has been inside a dark crevice for six months, and the sudden, bright sunlight stings its sensitive eyes. The snake basks in the sun for several hours, letting the heat warm its brown, speckled body. Soon, it will begin to make the slow-moving trek to an open field or woods, where it will spend the summer hunting for food and looking for a mate. Along the way, the wary rattlesnake will have to hide behind logs or big rocks, or in bushes or tall grass, and be careful not to get surprised by another animal or stepped on by a person. But even if that happens, a few shakes of its rattle should scare the creature off. Uncoiling its long, slender body, the rattlesnake sets out in search of its first meal of the season.

WHERE IN THE WORLD THEY LIVE

■ **Emerald Tree Boa**
Amazon Basin region of South America

■ **Yellow Anaconda**
South American countries of Brazil, Paraguay, Bolivia, and Argentina

■ **Garter Snake**
throughout North America to Central America

■ **Ball Python**
western and central Africa

□ **Cape Cobra**
southern Africa

■ **Blind Snake**
parts of Africa, Asia, South America, southern Central America, southwestern United States, northern Mexico

Numbering almost 3,000 species, snakes live on every continent of the world except Antarctica. While the great majority of snakes are found in tropical or subtropical regions, there are many Northern Hemisphere varieties as well. The colored squares represent some common locations of 11 snake species.

■ **Southern Pacific Rattlesnake**
southwestern California and Baja California

□ **Red-bellied Water Snake**
southeastern United States

■ **Milk Snake**
from southeastern Canada, throughout the United States, to northern South America

■ **Grass Snake**
England and throughout Europe

■ **Horned Viper**
North Africa, southern Europe, southwestern Africa, North American deserts

LEGLESS WONDERS

Because snakes are all muscle and have no limbs, most can coil up anywhere, even around small branches.

Snakes are some of the most widespread animals on Earth, and they are some of the most varied. There are more than 2,900 known species of snake, with new species being discovered every year. Snakes are reptiles, or **ectothermic** animals with backbones. Lizards are also reptiles, but unlike most lizards, snakes do not have limbs and are classified by the suborder Serpentes, meaning "serpents."

Within Serpentes, there are 18 families of snakes. These families can further be grouped into two sections: primitive snakes and true (or typical) snakes. Primitive snakes, such as blind snakes, worm snakes, and thread snakes, represent the earliest forms of snakes and lead the least complicated lives. True snakes, such as gopher snakes, rat snakes, king snakes, and most other snakes, are more **evolved** and more active.

Snakes look like lizards that do not have feet. Scientists think that snakes and lizards used to be the same creature until millions of years ago when snakes lost their limbs. However, some burrowing lizards are legless, and some snakes (such as boas) have tiny back leg claws. Lizards and snakes are still close relatives and share certain features, but the presence of shoulder bones sets lizards apart from snakes. Also, while both lizards and snakes have scales, snakes have only one row of scales along their bellies, while lizards have several rows.

Snakes live everywhere on Earth except the islands of Ireland, Iceland, and New Zealand, and the continent of Antarctica. Because snakes live in many different environments, the various species have developed their own adaptations to their climates and surroundings. Snakes are found in prairie grasses, forests, wetlands, deserts, high on mountaintops, and even in water. But the majority of snakes live in the tropical regions around the equator, where the temperature stays fairly warm, the air is always moist, and there are many animals to eat.

Unlike people and other mammals, snakes are ectotherms. To maintain an ideal body temperature of about 86 °F (30 °C), a snake lies in the sun to warm up and moves to the shade to cool down. In contrast, a mammal's blood is always warm and stays at a constant temperature, no matter what is happening in its environment. A snake's long body allows it to warm

Most snakes of the South American rainforests live on or under the ground, but some live in trees or the water.

All 61 species of the water-dwelling sea snake are poisonous, but the non-aggressive snakes rarely bite people.

up fast. If its body temperature falls too low, it becomes sluggish and cannot digest food properly. In cold climates, snakes conserve body heat by coiling up.

Both the area where a snake lives and its body size determine what it eats. All snakes are carnivorous, which means they eat meat. Snakes range in size from thread snakes, which are as short as four inches (10 cm) long and as thin as a straw, to giant anacondas, which can be more than 30 feet (9 m) long and can weigh 500 pounds (227 kg). Smaller snakes eat smaller animals such as insects, worms, small birds, and eggs; larger snakes eat larger animals such as rats, raccoons, other snakes, bats, and sometimes even deer and antelope. Large snakes such as boas and pythons can eat an animal three times their size.

Even though snakes have no outer ears, eyelids, or usable limbs, they manage to navigate their environments very well. Snakes have two eyes, one on each side of their head, but their eyesight is poor. Snakes instead rely on their ability to hear low-**frequency** sounds to keep themselves out of danger. As a snake moves along the ground, its jawbone picks up the

The small eyelash viper is a ferocious hunter, eating animals much larger than itself.

Snakes do not lap water like mammals do. They dunk their snouts underwater and use their throats to pump water into their stomachs.

vibrations made by movement and transfers the sound to the inner ears. If a snake detects footsteps from a person or large animal nearby, it has time to get away.

A snake's sense of smell is by far its most important sense. Snakes have two nostrils that detect scent particles in the air, but snakes stick out their forked tongue when they want to locate something such as a mate or dinner. Odor **molecules** in the air cling to the tongue, and when the snake pulls its tongue back in, the odors pass through two holes called the Jacobson's organ in the roof of its mouth, transferring the scent information to its brain. This allows a snake to find food, even in the dark.

All snakes have an inner skin and an outer skin. The outer skin is covered by dry scales made of keratin, a tough material that also makes up people's hair and fingernails. Even a snake's eyes are shielded by clear, thin scales called spectacles. **Pigments** in the scales give snakes their colors. Scales can be all the same color or made up of several colors, in striped or spotted patterns.

Every time a snake grows or its skin wears out, it molts, or sheds, its outer layer of skin. Usually, a snake

A boa constrictor's brown coloring with tan spots helps it blend in with the ground and trees in which it lives.

Although some rattlesnakes are sidewinders, the dangerous western diamondback rattlesnake is not.

rubs its head on an object, such as a rock, to loosen the skin around the mouth first. Then it pulls the rest of its body free, leaving the old skin behind. Adult snakes molt 3 or 4 times a year, while young snakes molt 6 to 12 times. Young snakes often shed their skin for the first time within a week of their birth.

Without limbs, a snake has to use its strong muscles to help it move. Some snakes move by pushing the sides of their bodies against surrounding objects or the ground. Others **contract** their muscles to crawl forward like caterpillars. Still others, such as tree snakes, move concertina-style: they push half of their body forward, then pull the rest of their body up, mimicking the motion of an accordion, or concertina, pumping. Sidewinding snakes, such as the horned viper, usually live in sandy, desert areas. To move forward, a sidewinder raises its head, bends the middle of its body into a loop, hurls its raised head and looped body into the air, then anchors itself with the front part of its body while lifting the rest off the sand to follow the same path. Small, thin snakes slither faster than large, heavy snakes, but the top speed of most snakes averages about three miles (4.8 km) per hour.

The European grass snake is a strong swimmer but does not live in the water all the time.

The amount of food a snake eats determines how often it can have babies. Arafura file snakes eat the least and lay eggs only once every decade.

Like other tropical tree snakes, green tree pythons make use of their slender, flexible bodies to wrap around trees.

ROAMING AND WAITING

Snakes' lives are not easy, but their bodies have adapted well to different habitats. In the water, the best swimmers are sea snakes and sea kraits, which live in both salt water and fresh water. These snakes have a special salt gland under their tongue that collects the salt from the water. Each time they flick their tongue, the gland pushes a small amount of the salt out before new water is taken in. Tree snakes have thin, pointed heads and tails that help them move through leaves and coil around branches in tropical rainforests. Other snakes such as thread snakes and blind snakes have hard, thick skulls and slick scales designed for burrowing underground.

Most snakes live in warm climates and are active throughout the year. But in deserts and other hot places, snakes may become **dormant** during the hottest and driest months. Snakes that live in cooler climates face a different dilemma when winter comes: how to keep warm when their bodies cannot create heat. Unlike birds or fast-moving mammals, snakes cannot **migrate** to warmer regions. When the temperature drops, snakes keep warm by finding a place such as a cave, barn, basement,

The Brahminy blind snake, or flowerpot snake, is the only snake species made up solely of females. It does not need to mate to produce babies.

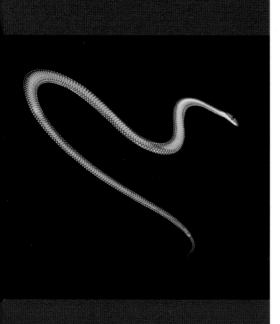

The Asian flying snake can glide through the air. After diving from a high branch, it pulls in its belly muscles to make itself into a parachute.

underground burrow, or deep crevice in which to make their dens. Inside the den, the snake hibernates—its heart rate and breathing slow down, its blood thickens, it stops growing, and it does not eat or drink. Hibernation can last from a few weeks to several months.

When spring comes, snakes slither out of their dens and begin looking for mates. By flicking its tongue, a male snake can detect the **pheromones** released by a female and determine if that snake will be a good mate. A male often mates with more than one female. In some species, such as the cobra, two males will wrestle and fight each other for the right to mate with a particular female. The mating season lasts for several weeks and occurs at different times for different species. After a male and female mate, each will go its own way.

The majority of snakes lay eggs, which are not hard but leathery and tough. Before laying her eggs, a female snake finds a warm, hidden place, such as in sand, an old log, or a pile of rotting leaves. The young develop inside the eggs for two to four months, then the mother lays her **clutch**, which usually consists of between 3 and 16 eggs. After laying the eggs, some mother snakes **incubate** them

for 55 days on average, or until they hatch, but other
mother snakes leave immediately and let the sun incubate
them. Once the mother has laid the eggs or after they
have hatched, mother and babies go their separate ways.
Snakes do not live in families.

About one-third of all snakes give birth to live young
instead of laying eggs. Baby snakes, called neonates,
develop in clear **membranes** inside the mother. The
membranes are filled with a nutrient-rich yolk, which the

*Female Indian cobras guard their
clutch of 12 to 20 eggs for the entire
50- to 60-day incubation period.*

Unlike most snakes, the female eyelash viper will stay with her young for about two months after giving birth.

babies eat to grow strong. When the babies are born, they are still inside the membranes and must use a temporary tooth called an egg tooth to cut themselves out of the membranes. After this happens, the mother leaves them. Young snakes know immediately how to hunt for food and defend themselves, acting on instinct. Snakes reach maturity, becoming able to mate, after two to four years.

A snake's food sources range from insects and spiders to porcupines and deer. Small tree- or ground-dwelling snakes use their tongues to follow the scent trails of prey such as spiders, birds, and other snakes. Bigger snakes, such as some boas, pythons, and pit vipers, have body heat-sensing organs called labial (lip) pits in their snouts. The labial pits allow them to sense if prey is close enough to eat or if a predator is nearby. Because these snakes have larger bodies and cannot move fast enough to catch up to prey, they lie partially hidden in a tree or on the ground, wait for prey to pass, then quickly ambush it. Because locating and catching prey can be difficult, most snakes eat as much as they can whenever they can. Snakes need to eat only 6 to 30 meals each year to be healthy.

When most poisonous snakes close their mouths, their fangs fold up against the roof. But coral snakes (above) have fixed fangs that do not fold.

To kill prey, snakes use any means necessary. Snakes have long, sharp, front teeth called fangs, which they use to stick into and hold on to prey. Large, thick snakes such as boas wrap themselves around prey to **constrict** the animal until it stops breathing. The jaws of most snakes can open very wide. This enables snakes to eat animals that are many times their own size. A snake hooks its back teeth into the animal, "walks" its mouth around it, and uses its throat muscles to pull the prey into its stomach.

About 600 species of the world's snakes are venomous, or poisonous. These snakes store venom above the fangs. When the snake bites, it injects venom through the fangs and into its victim. Sometimes the snake will poison an animal, release it, then follow its trail to find and eat it. Other times, the snake injects venom and holds on tight to the animal until the prey stops struggling and the snake can eat it.

Venomous snakes also use poison to defend themselves against predators such as birds, fish, foxes, coyotes, lions, and other snakes. When threatened, cobras will spit venom into the eyes of a predator to blind it, allowing the

Even small snakes can eat rodents and other creatures by grasping with their back teeth and widening their jaws.

cobras to escape. However, most snakes' best defense is to hide. A snake's coloring is often similar to its surroundings and helps **camouflage** it. Snakes with brightly-colored bands, such as the coral snake, are often poisonous, and their obvious colors warn off predators. The colors of some non-poisonous snakes often **mimic** the colors of poisonous ones to confuse predators and keep them away. When cornered, snakes hiss, writhe, or rattle their tails, as rattlesnakes do, to get predators to leave them alone. A snake usually bites in defense only when it feels threatened or provoked.

Indian snake charmers often perform outside public buildings, their cobras in a basket in front of them.

A HISTORY OF FEAR

Along with their connection to death and evil, the snakes in Medusa's hair also symbolized her wisdom.

Since people and snakes first interacted with each other millions of years ago, people have both feared and revered snakes. Snakes appear in some of the earliest known art carvings on stone and marble walls, which are at least 30,000 years old. Early on, snakes were represented as villains and connected with punishments. In the Bible, a story is told about how the Devil comes to Eve in the form of a snake and persuades her to eat an apple, which then dooms all people to a life of sin. In ancient Greece, a **myth** was told about a beautiful woman named Medusa who dared to compare her beauty to the goddess Athena's. As punishment, Athena turned Medusa's hair into a mass of writhing snakes, and anyone who looked directly at her was immediately turned to stone. Even in the 19th century, wily snakes were featured in stories such as Rudyard Kipling's *The Jungle Book*.

In contrast, ancient Romans believed that snakes brought good luck, so they often built shrines in which they could worship snakes and invited the creatures into their homes. The Aesculapian snake is named after the Greek god of healing, Asclepius (called Aesculapius in Latin, the language of the Romans). According to legend, the god Apollo sent a snake to teach Asclepius the medicinal value of plants. The Greeks also used the symbol of two snakes entwined around the staff of Hermes, the messenger god, as a sign for doctors. Today, physicians still use the same symbol.

The people of India have long had a fascination with the cobra. Snake charmers play flutelike instruments to charm cobras, or put them under a spell. Often, when the music starts, the cobra will lift its head and spread its hood of loose skin behind the head, which it does by expanding its ribs. Usually, cobras spread their hoods in defense or to show agitation. The cobra will then appear to sway to the music; it does not actually hear the music, but it follows the movements of the snake charmer and the shiny flute.

Despite their captivation with snakes, people have also feared snakes. In the 1600s, as people from Europe began to **colonize** North America, events called rattlesnake roundups were started to get rid of snakes in areas where people would settle. Cash prizes were offered to the person who killed the most rattlesnakes. Such fear-driven

destruction prompted zoologists in the 1800s to want to study snakes before they disappeared. They traveled around the world to collect huge numbers of snakes, ironically sometimes nearly eliminating certain local snake populations.

Snakes avoid contact with humans whenever possible. But when people try to catch a snake in the wild or happen upon a resting snake, they will often get bitten.

Australia's largest snake, the scrub python, is non-venomous but bites readily, posing a small threat to humans.

Australia is home to some of the world's most dangerous snakes. One bite from an inland taipan contains enough venom to kill 250,000 mice!

Today, several hundred thousand snakebites occur every year, and more than 20,000 result in death. Most of those deaths occur in Africa, Southeast Asia, and Central and South America, which have the greatest numbers of venomous snakes, poorer medical treatment, and more malnourished people. However, the number of deaths would be much higher without anti-venom treatment. Anti-venom was developed from snake venom in the late 1800s to treat poisonous snakebites. Today, less than one percent of treated bites in humans result in death.

Worldwide, snakes die from disease, starvation, predators, and accidents while hunting prey. But the biggest threat to snake survival is people. Human **encroachment** and other threats have recently caused more than 100 species to be declared endangered or threatened. Favorite habitats of snakes—such as forests, prairies, wetlands, and rainforests—are being cleared and replaced by homes, businesses, and highways. Although snakes generally stay away from cities and other urban areas, sometimes a city park, river, or stream will become a snake's home. These snakes are especially vulnerable to human activity.

Chemicals used in manufacturing, farming, and other industries have increased pollution of rivers, streams, and land, which in turn has made it difficult for snakes to live in those areas. Many scientists believe that pollution from factories, vehicle emissions, technological industries, and other human activities have helped to cause global warming, a gradual increase in Earth's temperature. Pollution and global warming have caused frogs, toads, salamanders, and other amphibians to die out in some places. Since many snakes feed on amphibians, a major food source is being depleted.

People still actively hunt snakes to kill them or to capture and sell them as pets. In China and other Asian countries, snake meat is considered a delicacy and is often eaten. In Australia and New Guinea, native people, known as Aborigines, are fond of eating snakes, especially pythons. People in some Asian countries also believe in a snake's healing powers, and snakes are often killed for use in traditional medicines. In Africa, Asia, and other areas where humans frequently come into contact with snakes, snakes are killed in self-defense or for sport.

Throughout time, people have worn clothes and

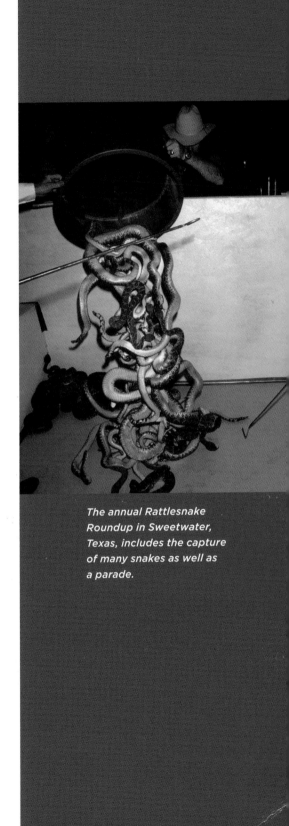

The annual Rattlesnake Roundup in Sweetwater, Texas, includes the capture of many snakes as well as a parade.

THE OUTSONG: KAA

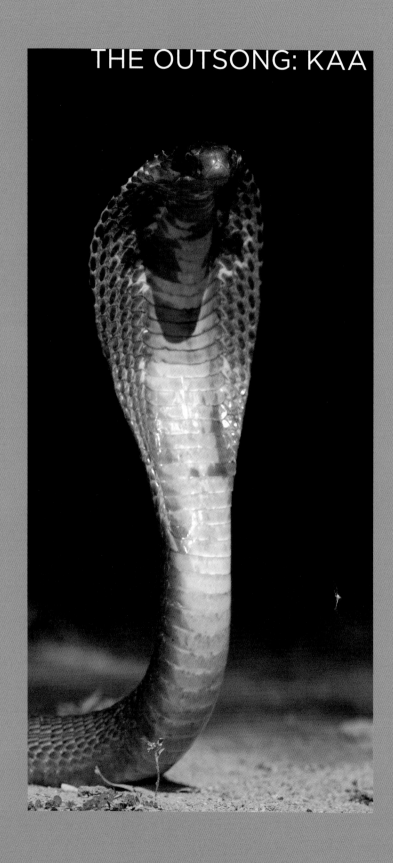

Anger is the egg of Fear—
Only lidless eyes see clear.
Cobra-poison none may leech—
Even so with Cobra-speech.
Open talk shall call to thee
Strength, whose mate is Courtesy.
Send no lunge beyond thy length.
Lend no rotten bough thy strength.
Gauge thy gape with buck or goat,
Lest thine eye should choke thy throat.
After gorging, wouldst thou sleep?
Look thy den be hid and deep,
Lest a wrong, by thee forgot,
Draw thy killer to the spot.
East and West and North and South,
Wash thy hide and close thy mouth.
(Pit and rift and blue pool-brim,
Middle-Jungle follow him!)
Wood and Water, Wind and Tree,
Jungle-Favour go with thee!

Rudyard Kipling (1865–1936)
from The Jungle Book

shoes made of snakeskin, and snakeskin goods are more fashionable than ever today. Each year, millions of snakes are killed to make shoes, purses, belts, and coats. In the 1990s, the popularity of keeping snakes such as boas and pythons as pets soared. Millions of snakes and snake products are shipped and sold worldwide each year.

Starting in the 1960s, wildlife societies such as the Humane Society of the United States began to educate people about the importance of snakes. Biologists and **herpetologists** worked with volunteers and staff at zoos and wildlife centers such as those run by the Wildlife Conservation Society and the World Wildlife Fund to make people aware of the necessity of preserving snake populations. Many threatened species in North America, such as the San Francisco garter snake and the Alameda whip snake, are now protected by law. In recent years, nature magazines such as *National Geographic* have featured many articles about snakes, which has made people take a new interest in the plight of snakes. Many people now see snakes as beautiful, exotic creatures instead of evil animals. Yet most people continue to be prejudiced against snakes.

Like its threatened North American relative the Alameda whip snake, the green whip snake has a long, slender body.

Fossils of sand boas found in Wyoming suggest that these snakes lived in the area about 32 million years ago.

MORE TO DISCOVER

A lthough people have been fascinated by snakes for millennia, only within the past 200 years have researchers thoroughly begun to study the snake's form and habitat. Today, scientists routinely venture into the most remote parts of the world to capture snakes in order to learn more about them. Through their findings, people everywhere have the opportunity to study these unique creatures.

More than 380 million years ago, primitive amphibians called Labrynthodonts roamed the earth. Amphibians are vertebrates, or animals with backbones, that have soft outer skins and live on land and in water. Eighty million years later, reptiles such as crocodiles and lizards developed from these early amphibians. Reptiles were the first vertebrate animals to live entirely on land.

The first snakes are believed to have evolved 150 to 100 million years ago from lizard ancestors. As time passed, Earth's climate and waters changed, and animal species had to adapt to survive. Because snakes have poor vision, they are thought to have developed from lizards that burrowed underground and thus had no need for

The physical resemblances between lizards and snakes are plainly seen, from the scales to the body shape.

A snake's venom, produced by glands below and behind the eyes, travels out of the body through the fangs.

good eyesight. Scientists believe the first snakes had legs; males of a few species today still have tiny back legs called spurs that are used in fighting and mating. Burrowing, however, was much easier without legs, and snakes are thought to have lost their legs in order to burrow into the ground and fit inside small crevices.

When snakes first evolved, some scientists think that the continents of South America, Africa, and Australia were joined together as one landmass, while the continents of North America, Europe, and Asia formed another. As these lands separated into different continents about 60 million years ago, the world's snake population redistributed itself. This theory helps explain why today's North American snakes are closely related to those in Europe and Asia, while South American snakes resemble those in Africa and Australia.

Snakes benefit nature and people in many ways, and their total destruction would have far-reaching negative consequences. By feeding on spiders, insects, and rodents, snakes prevent these animals from invading homes and spreading disease. They also help protect crops from being devoured by insects and small mammals. Scientists

The smaller of the two anaconda species, the yellow anaconda can behave unpredictably when in captivity.

are also discovering that a snake's venom can be used for medicinal purposes to treat diseases and pain in humans.

Worldwide, an increasing number of organizations and individuals are becoming dedicated to preserving snake species. Many zoos around the world hold snakes in captivity and provide them with environments that resemble their natural habitats; snake and other reptile exhibits are some of the most-visited in many zoos. Snakes

The snakes that slither the fastest often have striped bodies. The stripes make it hard to see that the snake is moving at all.

in the wild live an average of 20 years, and captive snakes often live 3 or 4 years longer, thanks to help from humans. As the popularity of keeping snakes as pets has increased, amateur herpetological societies have also increased in number to teach people firsthand how to treat snakes and how snakes and humans can peacefully coexist.

Young people learn about snakes through books, the Internet, and visits to nature centers, and many are coming to appreciate and even like snakes. In the 1930s, Boy Scouts in the U.S. received bronze medals for killing northern water snakes, believing they would be protecting nearby trout populations by doing so. Now, many children learn the importance of valuing snakes for their role in the animal kingdom and want to protect snakes instead.

Nature centers often give people a close-up look at snakes, which leads to a better appreciation of them. Inside the Narcisse Wildlife Management Area in Manitoba, Canada, thousands of garter snakes awaken from hibernation every April and May and pour like water out of their dens. The garter snake awakening has become a tourist attraction at Narcisse, and each year, hundreds of people and busloads of children come to see and hold the harmless garter snakes.

People can provide snakes with some of the best chances they have for survival through agreeing to treaties such as the Convention on International Trade in Endangered Species, or CITES, which was signed in Washington, D.C., in 1973. The agreement, which had been adopted by 173 countries as of 2008, regulates international trading of threatened species, including many types of snakes, and the products made from them. CITES has led to some species of snakes increasing in population, but many countries lack the law enforcement to uphold agreements such as CITES. Perhaps an even stronger method for protecting snakes lies in the hands of local branches of groups such as the Nature Conservancy and the National Audubon Society.

Today, many regions of the world are actively trying to protect snakes. The state of Arizona guards its endangered small rattlesnake species and jails any **poachers** that are caught. In the African country of Uganda, the 127-square-mile (329 sq km) Bwindi Impenetrable National Park is home to hundreds of snake species as well as many

Reserves such as Bwindi Impenetrable National Park protect animals such as gorillas in addition to snakes.

rare animals such as mountain gorillas. In Brazil, certain wilderness reserves, which the government has set aside as land for native peoples, are also home to many species of snakes, protecting them from additional human contact. When humans such as ranchers do pose a threat to snakes that live in the same areas where their cattle graze, though, other actions must be taken to help snakes survive. The Malpai Borderlands Group, based in Arizona, educates ranchers on how to conserve more grassland for native species such as New Mexico ridge-nosed rattlesnakes instead of destroying snake habitats through overgrazing.

The battle to save snake habitats from human encroachment is only just beginning, but people are determined to do what they can to save this sometimes exotic creature. Every year, new species and even new characteristics about existing species are discovered. At the same time, though, people spread out and continue to overtake snakes' natural habitats. But the more people learn about the lives of snakes, the better the chance that these unique animals will continue to hold their place as some of the most adaptable, fascinating, and mysterious creatures in the world.

Even with their reputation for causing harm, snakes continue to be intriguing subjects for people to study.

ANIMAL TALE: DJISDAAH AND THE BATTLE WITH THE SNAKES

For hundreds of years, American Indian tribes such as the Iroquois lived and worked among many kinds of snakes. They probably witnessed a snake defend itself by biting a person, and that person might have tried to get back at the snake. The following story teaches why it is important to treat snakes with respect.

In the village there lived a man named Djisdaah who was not kind to animals. One day when he was hunting, he found a rattlesnake and decided to torture it. He held its head to the ground and pierced it with a piece of bark. He did this to other snakes, too.

One day, another man from his village was walking through the forest when he heard a strange sound, louder than the wind hissing through the tops of tall pine trees. He crept closer to see. There, in a great clearing, were many snakes. They were gathered for a war council, and as the man listened in fright, he heard them say:

"We shall now fight with them. Djisdaah has challenged us, and we shall go to war. In four days, we shall go to their village and fight them."

The man crept away and then ran as fast as he could to tell his village what he had heard and seen. The chief sent other men to see if the report was true. They returned in great fright.

"Ahh," they said, "it is so. The snakes are all gathering to have a war."

The chief of the village could see that he had no choice. "We must fight," he said, and ordered the people of the village to

make preparations for battle. They cut mountains of wood and stacked it in long piles all around the village. They built rows of stakes close together to keep the snakes out. When the fourth day came, the chief ordered that the piles of wood be set on fire.

Usually a snake will not go near a fire, but these snakes were determined to have their revenge. They went straight into the flames. Some of them died, but many others lived. The snakes were more numerous than the men, and they could not be stopped.

It was now clear to the chief of the village that his warriors could never win this battle. He shouted to the snakes that had reached the edge of the village: "Hear me, my brothers. We surrender to you. We have done you a great wrong. Have mercy on us."

The snakes stopped where they were, and there was a great silence. The exhausted warriors looked at the great army of snakes, and the snakes stared back at them. Then the earth trembled and cracked in front of the humans. A great snake, a snake taller than the biggest pine tree, whose head was larger than a great longhouse, lifted himself out of the hole in the earth.

"Hear me," he said. "I am the chief of all the snakes. We shall go and leave you in peace if you will agree to one thing."

The chief of the warriors looked at the great snake and nodded his head. "We will agree, Great Chief," he said.

"It is well," said the Chief of the Snakes. "This is the one thing: you must always treat my people with respect."

GLOSSARY

camouflage – the ability to hide, due to coloring or markings that blend in with a given environment

clutch – a group of eggs produced and incubated at the same time

colonize – to establish settlements in a new land and exercise control over them

constrict – to make smaller or narrower by binding or squeezing

contract – to draw muscles together, becoming shorter or tighter in order to cause movement

dormant – in a resting state during which physical functions are slowed down

ectothermic – having a body temperature that is dependent on external heat sources (such as the sun)

encroachment – movement into the space of another

evolved – gradually developed into a new form

frequency – the measurement of sound waves

herpetologists – scientists who study reptiles and amphibians

incubate – to keep an egg warm and protected until it is time for it to hatch

membranes – thin, clear layers of tissue that cover internal organs or developing limbs

migrate – to travel from one region or climate to another for feeding or breeding purposes

mimic – to copy or imitate closely; to take on the appearance of another living thing

molecules – groups of small particles called atoms that are attached to each other and form chemical compounds

myth – a popular or traditional belief or story that explains how something came to be or that is associated with a person or object

pheromones – chemicals given off by animals that influence the behavior or development of others of the same species, often functioning to attract males to females

pigments – materials or substances present in the tissues of animals or plants that gives them their natural coloring

poachers – people who hunt protected species of wild game and fish, even though doing so is against the law

SELECTED BIBLIOGRAPHY

Badger, David. *Snakes*. Edited by Gretchen Bratvold. Stillwater, Minn.: Voyageur Press, 1999.

Bauchot, Roland, ed. *Snakes: A Natural History*. New York: Sterling Publishing Company, 1994.

Kidzone. "Snake Facts." DLTK's Sites. http://www.kidzone.ws/lw/snakes/facts.htm.

Greene, Harry W. *Snakes: The Evolution of Mystery in Nature*. Berkeley, Calif.: University of California Press, 1997.

Hutchins, Michael, James B. Murphy, and Neil Schlager, eds. *Grzimek's Animal Life Encyclopedia*, 2nd ed. Vol. 7, *Reptiles*. Farmington Hills, Mich.: Gale Group, 2003.

Mattison, Chris. *The New Encyclopedia of Snakes*. Princeton, N.J.: Princeton University Press, 2007.

Great Basin rattlesnakes, common in the western United States, are often found on warm rock outcroppings.

INDEX